THE POWER OF A NEW BEGINNING

'LANRE SOMORIN MD

THE POWER OF A NEW BEGINNING

'LANRE SOMORIN MD

PUBLISHING
Little Rock
2018

Copyright 2018 by 'Lanre Somorin, M.D.
Published by Faith 2 Fe Publishing Company
Little Rock, Arkansas 72205
Printed in the United States of America

ISBN-13: 978-0-9989377-5-5

Printed in the United States of America. All rights reserved under International Copyright Law. No part of this publication may be reproduced, stored in a retrieval system or transmitted in any form or by any means-electronic, mechanical, photocopy, recording or any other- except for brief quotations in printed reviews, without the prior written permission of the author.

Unless otherwise noted, all scripture is from the King James Version of the Bible.

Scripture quotations marked AMPC are from *The Amplified Bible*, Old Testament ©1965,1987 by the Zondervan Corporation. The Amplified New Testament© 1958,1987 by The Lockman Foundation,

Scripture quotations marked MSG are from *The Message*. Copyright ©1993, 1995 by Eugene H. Peterson. Used by permission of NavPress Publishing Group

Scriptures marked as GNT are taken from the Good News Translation -Second Edition © 1992 by American Bible Society. Used by permission.

Scripture quotations marked GW are from *God's Word,* a work of God's Word to the Nations, © 1995 by God's Word to the Nations. Quotations arc used by permission.

Scripture quotations marked NASB are from the New American Standard Bible ®, © 1960, 1962, 1963, 1968, 1971, 1972, 1973, 1975, 1977, 1995 by The Lockman Foundation. Used by permission.

Scripture quotations marked NIV are from The Holy Bible, New International Version © 1973, 1978, 1984 by the International Bible Society. Used by permission of Zondervan Publishing House.

Scripture quotations marked NKJ Version are from the New King James Version © 1982 by Thomas Nelson Inc.

Scripture quotations marked TLB are from *The Living Bible,* copyright © 1971. Used by permission of Tyndale House Publishers, Inc., Wheaton, Illinois 60189. All rights reserved.

Table of Contents

Introduction iii
1. Transition to Greater 1
2. Identify the Hindrances 9
3. Steps Toward a New Beginning 13
4. God's Provision for Your New Beginning 27
5. The Power of Self-Discipline 41
6. The Greater One Is in You 47
7. Take Control of Your Destiny 57

Introduction

The Bible says "Eye hath not seen, nor ear heard, neither have entered into the heart of man, the things which God hath prepared for them that love him. But God hath revealed them unto us by his Spirit" (First Cor. 2:9-10 KJV).

We are not supposed to wander through life, not knowing what God is doing. We need to seek Him to know what direction He is going; we need to stick with that, to see the blessing in our lives.

We should not be coming up with our own plan, and then asking for God's blessing. We should be seeking His plan, because it is already blessed.

He is able to do exceedingly, abundantly, above all we ask or think, according to the power that works in us (Eph. 3:20). Whatever you are thinking, God is able to do exceedingly above that. God does not want us to remain in the same place from year to year; He wants to move us further along in His plan for our lives.

He wants to make what is barren to be fruitful, and what is fruitful to multiply. What areas of your life have been barren in previous years? God wants to bring fruitfulness to them.

What areas have been fruitful? God wants to bring multiplication to them. He is the God of a new beginning. God does not want us to be static.

We are moving forward, and God is accelerating us!

There will be fulfilled expectations because we are not going to remain in the same place. We won't say, "Different year, same problems." We won't just grow older.

God has certain things in store for us. At one point He said to me, "There is a certain thing I am doing in you that is destined to go from small to great. Are you positioned to recognize it?"

Job 8:7 says "Though thy beginning was small, yet thy latter end should greatly increase." It doesn't matter how you started, your latter end shall increase abundantly.

There is something in your life that is destined to grow from small to great. Are you positioned to recognize it? For you to have fulfillment, you must have expectation. God wants us to have expectation. God is doing something new in our lives, and it is important that we recognize it.

The goal of this book is to help you cooperate with what God is doing in your life. It is to help you recognize the new thing He is doing.

He may want to resurrect an area that you considered dead. He may want to expand or multiply an area that is doing well. Or, He may want you to begin something in a completely new area.

Whatever God is impressing on your heart, my prayer is that you will align yourself with it, because His plan is already blessed!

Chapter 1

Transition to Greater

Be alert to what God is saying. Myles Monroe once said, "There is something for you to start that it is ordained for you to finish."[1]

Isaiah 60:22 says, "A little one shall become a thousand, and a small one a strong nation." I am always fascinated to see how businesses go from small to great. Everyone starts small. What are the things or principles involved in going from small to great?

One of the things God told me to focus on when I prayed about the coming year was to mind my own business. God was telling me to focus on my private practice. I owned and operated a state-licensed rehab clinic from 2010 to 2016 and employed several people.

The facility was subject to state regulations and policies regarding hiring and other things. It was always exciting to look for ways to grow it and make it go from small to great. I also had a private behavioral health practice but chose to put it to the side during this period because the rehab clinic took so much of my time.

After closing the rehab clinic, becoming involved with anything that had overhead seemed unappealing, so I reluctantly continued my private practice in Monroe, New York. It seemed more comfortable to do consultations at other sites and not grow my practice at its primary location.

I did not want to repeat the same mistakes as with the clinic. The clinic's overhead was too much. It soon became apparent that I was being too cautious with my practice.

I decided to get a job with much bigger responsibilities and more pay; however, it was still another person's organization. After a year or two, God began to say, "You need to focus on your business."

I said, "Okay." There comes a point where you do something well or you shut it down, and I came to that place in 2017. My practice was just making enough money to stay open.

The Lord also told me to publish and to put emphasis on my first book, *Seize Your Moment (Unmasking Everyday Opportunities)*. Once the book had been published, I needed a website.

I had created a website for my business, but it needed to be updated. A notice on the existing website simply said, "This rehab is closed. We are moving to a new location." The notice had been up for two years! It was dormant.

God told me to pick up my practice again. I had paid to have a logo created, but hadn't used it in seven years. The previous web designer said she would charge me $50.00 to retrieve it from the archives.

Is there something you have pushed to the side?

Is there something you have considered dead?

God may want to breathe life into it. The web designer did a fantastic job of revitalizing the website. The website is now connected to my book, and my book has created interest in the website. My practice is growing, opportunities for consultation are increasing, and so are responsibilities on my new job. I have seen significant growth in the practice, and significant sales for the first book.

God is going to do something new. Are you going to see it? Are you going to recognize it? Let's begin with the following verse.

> *Behold, I will do a new thing; now it shall spring forth; shall ye not know it? I will even make a way in the wilderness, and rivers in the desert.* Isaiah 43:19

The same verse in the Message Translation says:

> *Be alert, be present. I'm about to do something brand-new. It's bursting out! Don't you see it? There it is! I'm making a road through the desert, rivers in the badlands.* Isaiah 43:19 MSG

In the Good News Translation, this verse says:

> *But the Lord says, Watch for the new thing I am going to do. It is happening already—you can see it now! I will make a road through the wilderness and give you streams of water there.* Isaiah 43:19 GNT

The Amplified Bible, Classic Edition says:

> *Behold, I am doing a new thing! Now it springs forth; do you not perceive and know it and will you not give heed to it? I will even make a way in the wilderness and rivers in the desert.* Isaiah 43:19 (AMPC)

Sometimes we say that God wants to do a new thing, but we don't know what that new thing is. God says, "…do you not perceive *and* know it *and* will you not give heed to it?" Isaiah

43:19 (AMPC). If you don't know what that new thing is, how will you give heed to it?

You cannot go through the year aimlessly, hoping something good will just happen. God will tell you and show you what He wants to do; or, He will at least help prepare you for it.

In First Corinthians 2:9-10 it says, "But as it is written, Eye hath not seen, nor ear heard, neither have entered into the heart of man, the things which God hath prepared for them that love him. But God hath revealed them unto us by his Spirit."

> You need to perceive what the Lord is doing, to know it, and to give heed to it.

You need to perceive what the Lord is doing, to know it, and to give heed to it. Proverbs 29:18 (NLT) says, "When people do not accept divine guidance, they run wild. But whoever obeys the law is joyful." The King James Version says, "Where there is no vision, the people perish." The NIV says, "Where there is no revelation, people cast off restraint."

You need to be able to perceive what God is doing in the church, and what He is saying in your own life. When you don't perceive it, the year just runs along.

You need to know it.

Knowing is a deeper level of perception. The Amplified Bible says in Proverbs 29:18 "Where there is no vision [no revelation of God and His word], the people are unrestrained; But happy *and* blessed is he who keeps the law [of God]."

You have to know what God is doing and what He is doing in you. Then, you have to give heed to it.

> *The path of the righteous is like the morning sun, shining ever brighter till the full light of day. But*

the way of the wicked is like deep darkness; they do not know what makes them stumble. Proverbs 4:18-19 (NIV)

When your rearview mirror becomes your windshield, you are destined for a life of mediocrity and stagnation. When you look at your present and your future through your past, you are going nowhere.

There is a reason your windshield is huge, and your rearview mirror is very small.[2] A windshield is huge because you need to be able to scan everywhere. A rearview mirror is just a small mirror for you to take an occasional glance at. You cannot stare at your rearview mirror and drive.

Many people live their lives looking at their rearview mirrors. If someone proposes something to them, they say, "Oh, I did that once. I remember it well. I got burned."

When you have vision, you need to know who you should have around you. Sometimes a person who has become your best friend is really a distraction.

If you are doing things and not getting the results you want, you are living a life of darkness. That is not what God has called you to do.

The Bible says the life of the righteous is meant to get brighter and brighter. If you have not reached full brightness yet, then more brightness is expected. Your future is bright! Your future is getting brighter!

My son, pay attention to my words. Open your ears to what I say. Do not lose sight of these things. Keep them deep within your heart because they are life to those who find them and they heal the whole body. Guard your heart more than anything else, because the source of your life flows from it. Remove dishonesty from your mouth. Put deceptive speech far away from your lips. Let your eyes look straight ahead and your sight be focused in front of you. Carefully walk a straight path, and all your ways will be secure. Do not lean to the right or to the left. Walk away from evil. Proverbs 4:20:20-27 (GW)

You need to have vision. You need to give heed to what God is doing. You may not feel that you have a prophetic revelation, but you still have expectations.

God has a vision to prosper you so much that you will be able to be a blessing. God's vision is not just for the local church; God has a vision for me and you. All these visions are connected. God "is able to do exceeding abundantly above all that we ask or think" (Eph. 3:20 KJV).

How do you get from where you are to where God wants you to be? You need to know God's vision for your life. You need to take time to perceive what God is saying to you. *My soul, wait thou only upon God; for my expectation* is *from him* (Psalm 62:5 KJV).

God is paying attention to your expectation. What is your expectation? God wants to make this a year of fulfilled expectations.

God began to speak to me about what He wanted to do; He said it would be like the difference between flying and driving below the speed limit. I would need to put road markers in my year at the end of each quarter to see the advances God was going to make.

Transition to Greater

An airplane begins to move, it accelerates and gains speed, and then, it takes off. You should not still be on the tarmac in November.

In Genesis 26:13 (NKJV) God says of Isaac, "The man began to prosper, and continued prospering until he became very prosperous." What are the signs in my life of "beginning to prosper"? Determine what you are trusting God to accomplish in the first quarter of your year.

Chapter 2

Identify the Hindrances

Let's investigate some hindrances in your life. We want to identify hindrances to a new beginning.

THE HINDRANCE OF DISTRACTION

The first hindrance is distraction. You may be so busy day-to-day that you don't take note of what you are accomplishing for the week. You may feel that you don't have time to think about the vision you have for your life. You may be just trying to get through "today." Are you going minute-by-minute, day-by-day?

You cannot live your life in crisis mode. Step back! You must have a vision for your life. Where are you headed? How will you get there?

In terms of planning, you should have goals for the week, for the month, and for the year. Take time to look at your life. At a minimum, you should be regularly evaluating your life to be sure you are not making the same mistakes over and over.

At this point, we are not talking about coming up with a 10-year or a 15-year goal. Look at your life, and see how you lived this past week. Reflect on your day, on your week. What things would you like to do differently so you are not making the same mistakes over and over again? That is the minimum you should be doing.

THE HINDRANCE OF DELEGATION

The second hindrance is delegation. This hindrance can occur when you have given control of your life over to someone else or to chance. You may say, "It is out of my hands. God is going to do it. If this is my year, it is going to happen."

I asked someone, "How are you doing?"

He said, "Well, my mood depends on my girlfriend. If she is doing well, I am great. If *she* is not doing well, *I* am not doing well."

To whom have you delegated your well-being? Your girlfriend or boyfriend should not control your mood. You must control your mood.

If you delegate this, the enemy will not need to attack you directly. He will only need to attack the person you delegated your life to. All he needs to do is cause indirect influence.

Do not delegate your joy and peace to someone; this includes your spouse, your boss, your pastor, any leader, or even your children. Why do people permit their spouse to have total control over their lives? God doesn't consult another person when He wants to give us direction.

Someone may ask, "How are you?" Do you need to send a text to someone to find out? That person is dealing with his or her own life. Are you going to make another person responsible for hearing God and telling you what He said?

Some people leave their life to chance. If it happens, okay. If not, okay. They may be waiting for their pastor to give a prophetic word. You need to get your own prophetic word.

Identify the Hindrances

THE HINDRANCE OF DISILLUSIONMENT

The next hindrance is disillusionment. This hindrance takes place when you allow past events to make you think, *This is as good as it gets* or *This is the best God has for me.*

Everyone's expectation is shaped a good deal by what has happened to them in the past.

You may look at people around you and realize that none of them have become successful or rich. That may condition you against success and wealth. You have to determine how much of that information you are going to allow to shape where you are today.

Many people do things the way they have always been done without investigating why they are that way. People allow themselves to become conditioned by observing other people's mistakes or mediocrity.

God can do exceedingly, abundantly more than you can ask or think; isn't that what we say when we go to church? The same anointing that we have at church is on you every day.

Why not ask God to help you create something exceedingly, abundantly above all that you ask or think?

Why do we limit the anointing? God created us for more than mere survival.

THE HINDRANCE OF DISEMPOWERMENT

Another hindrance is disempowerment. Disempowerment means you are not giving yourself the power to decide about your future. As you continue to hesitate, you will feel more and more restricted.

The Power of a New Beginning

The result is that you are unable to take responsibility for your future. This leads to prolonged indecision and coasting. You will then become immobilized. The outcome of this process is that you will have a morbid fear of making a decision, and you will make no attempt to improve your life.

We need to overcome distraction, delegation, disillusionment, and disempowerment.

Chapter 3

Steps Toward a New Beginning

Let's investigate some steps we need to take toward a new beginning. The steps to a new beginning are planning, revelation and insight, and obedience to instruction.

STEP ONE: PLANNING

> *The preparations of the heart belong to man, But the answer of the tongue is from the Lord.* Proverbs 16:1 NKJV

The first step to a new beginning is planning. You need to be able to see what God is doing. Once you see what God is doing, you need to begin to prepare for it. The miracle happens when you are where you are supposed to be when the miracle comes.

Be ready when opportunity comes your way! Stop having a short-term vision for your life and start thinking of the long-term impact of decisions you are making today.

The preparation of the heart belongs to man. There is preparation that needs to happen. See what God is doing and understand it.

STEP TWO: REVELATION AND INSIGHT

It is important that we have revelation and insight. God will give you specific revelation on what you need to do.

For instance, God told me to pay attention to my business, to decrease spending, and focus on my book. I wrote these things down, so I could concentrate on them. I meditated on what God was telling me. I looked at each month in advance and asked, "What are the danger points?" I was used to spending excessively. What triggered that?

Budget experts tell us to find out exactly what we are spending money on each month. People say, "The devil is in the details." Well, I want to tell you that the blessing is in the details! Get detailed about what God is telling you to do. Break it all down so you know what steps to take.

Learn to appreciate and measure small changes. You cannot move forward until you know where you are and where God wants you to be. This helps you know the season you are in, and it helps you discern God's will for your life.

> *If any of you lack wisdom, let him ask of God, that giveth to all men liberally, and upbraideth not; and it shall be given him.* James 1:5

Unfortunately, the last thing people seek when they are in trying circumstances is wisdom.

What people want is to get out of the circumstance, and for the circumstance to go away. If you get a bad grade, you just want the pain of the bad grade to go away.

Seldom do people try to see what caused it. They should ask, "What went wrong here? What can I do differently next time?"

Steps Toward a New Beginning

When God tells us what to focus on, we need to do it. I began to break down the metrics and determined what I needed to focus on each week and each month. I had been too busy doing other things to take care of my website.

Wisdom is time and energy in the right direction. Concerning my practice, I needed to learn about insurance, know who was scheduled for appointments, and who was missing appointments. God told me to have a conference call with my biller every month and break everything down; I needed to look at the smallest details. I focused on the billing and applied the wisdom of God to that certain area. Change was happening!

Wisdom helps you know the season you are currently living in. If you lack wisdom, you ask. Wisdom enables you to use the right amount of time and energy in the right direction for maximum results.

> Wisdom enables you to use the right amount of time and energy in the right direction for maximum results.

Some people tell me they are trying to get a job. Why do they have people praying for them every three months to get a new job? They say, "Well, I'm just not going to take it. They (referring to their bosses) talked to me the wrong way." They are not going to take the paycheck, either. If a person has the favor of God on his life, but he lacks people skills, he is going nowhere.

Proverbs 3:5-6 says, "Trust in the Lord with all thine heart; and lean not unto thine own understanding. In all thy ways acknowledge him, and he shall direct thy paths." If you need help, acknowledge Him! Get wisdom! Get direction!

As I made plans to launch my book, I was told I needed someone to help with social networking. Someone had come to our church to give a presentation on social media networking and marketing. I thought, *I should have come to one of those classes!* The resources I needed had been available all the time! Resources are available for you! The key to understanding is knowledge.

> *If the axe is dull and he does not sharpen its edge, then he must exert more strength. Wisdom has the advantage of giving success.* Ecclesiastes 10:10 NASB

Wisdom brings success. "If the axe is dull…" What does that mean? If you don't have current information, you end up working harder and longer. You go around in circles. When you invest in skill development, your time is at a premium.

Learn what you don't know. Some people rely on the idiom which says, "What you don't know can't hurt you." That is a lie. What you don't know is hurting you right now. You are just not aware it is. You don't know what you don't know.

One of my goals is to take advantage of medical conferences and to learn all I can. I want to be at the cutting edge. That will help me in my practice. For example, I recently attended a conference in Sarasota that was sponsored by the Mayo Clinic. After that, I went to a weekend conference at NYU.

On the following Monday after the NYU conference, I was able to utilize information I learned there. A colleague called to ask if I knew how to handle a complex problem concerning a medication. The colleague is a neurologist and a psychiatrist. The answer he needed was in my conference notes. I said, "I have that right here."

The doctor said, "Man, you are smart!"

Stay on the cutting edge. Watch your current habits. Watch your eating habits. Watch your spending habits. Watch your saving habits. Watch your work habits.

Steps Toward a New Beginning

Recently, I went to the doctor because I was having pain in my leg. I was told to get on the scale. I was shocked to learn I had gained weight in the past year. I did not change my eating habits, but my body was reacting differently because I am older now. I was initially in denial about my weight. I refused to believe I weighed that much.

However, I have a wife who brings me out of denial. I told her what my weight was, and she said, "Yes. I know." I sought her help. I used to eat rice for lunch for the past 10 years or more. She got me on a better diet and exercise regimen. Now, I am taking salads to work.

One morning, my wife asked me if I preferred croissants or oatmeal for breakfast. I said, "I will take oatmeal, please, and two boiled eggs."

She said, "Didn't you have two eggs yesterday? What is your cholesterol? Is it borderline, or over?" So, my wife is watching my diet.

I said, "Forget the boiled eggs. I will stick with the oatmeal."

After taking salad to work for two weeks, and not eating late at night, I weighed myself. I was excited! I had begun to lose the weight. You need to be able to appreciate small changes, and to know that small changes will lead to incremental changes over time. Wisdom!

My pastor told an anecdote several years ago about a plumber. The plumber was called to a company that was having problems with a boiler. He assessed the situation, then took out a hammer and tapped the boiler in a certain spot. Then, it worked perfectly.

When he presented his bill, he wanted $400.00. The owner of the company was amazed, and asked, "Why should it cost $400.00? All you did was tap the boiler." The plumber answered.

"Tapping the boiler costs zero. Knowing where to tap the boiler costs $400.00."[1]

We can all say, "We need to make a change." That is not the issue. The issue for you is what change do you need to make? Invest in knowledge in your field.

The blessing is in the details! God has a plan. What does He want to resurrect in your life? You may have put that aside because of past hurts and disappointments and failures.

You may be thinking, *anything else but that!* God wants to resurrect something. He wants a new beginning, and He wants to equip you for it.

You need to recognize the steps God wants you to take as He is moving you from small to great.

STEP THREE: OBEDIENCE TO INSTRUCTION

> *And it came to pass, that, as the people pressed upon him to hear the word of God, he stood by the lake of Gennesaret, And saw two ships standing by the lake: but the fishermen were gone out of them, and were washing their nets. And he entered into one of the ships, which was Simon's, and prayed him that he would thrust out a little from the land. And he sat down, and taught the people out of the ship. Now when he had left speaking, he said unto Simon, Launch out into the deep, and let down your nets for a draught. And Simon answering said unto him, Master, we have toiled all the night, and have taken nothing: nevertheless at thy word I will let down the net. And when they had this done, they inclosed a great multitude of fishes: and their net brake. Luke 5:1-6*

Steps Toward a New Beginning

Many of you are familiar with the story of Peter. He had toiled all night and caught no fish. His expertise had told him when to fish, where to fish, and how to do it. He was diligent in his work. You may have done something as well as you know how, but it hasn't succeeded.

God told Peter to take the same tools and the same expertise and begin again. Peter didn't change his partners or his boat. The only thing Peter changed was direction.

He may have wanted to throw his boat away, throw his nets away, change his partners, and then look for another place to fish.

God began to show me the things in my life that needed my closer attention. Because of the failure of a similar business, I didn't want anything to do with that *line* of business. I still had reams of paper in my basement from the failed business that I had forgotten about. I realized I could use them in my private practice.

God may want you to use the same tools, the same line of business, and the same partners, but shift direction and shift focus. I remembered the paper. It had been sitting for two years gathering dust. Are we going to listen to God?

Jesus told Peter to launch out into the deep and let down his nets (plural) for a catch. Peter only let down one net. He obeyed Jesus, but his was partial obedience. The increase that came was net-breaking.

Thank God he didn't let go of his partners, because he had to ask them for help. When the fish are in the net, it is not the time to look for partners.

All he needed was direction and instruction from God. More importantly, he did what God asked him to do. Peter used the same tools.

My business increased, and I needed to hire some employees to help me. I resisted that because I previously had a high payroll before and I didn't want another one. I had to convince myself to increase the hours of my part-time secretary. I was overly cautious.

When someone offers you an opportunity, you want it to come with a guarantee, but it does not happen that way.

Jesus said, "Launch out into the deep, and let down your nets for a catch." Peter had a decision to make. Peter decided to obey Jesus' instructions even when his mind was telling him something different.

Sometimes we think we should do something entirely different from our area of expertise. God wanted to resurrect something old, but in a new way. Be open to whatever God tells us to do.

There may be certain areas of our lives that we have designated "no-go" areas. We think the resurrection power of God is not strong enough to resurrect them. We think they are dead! Consider David as an example. When Samuel asked David's father how many sons he had, he didn't even think of David.

> God's blessings are connected to our obedience to His instructions.

Peter decided to obey, but in his own way. How many times does God tell us to do something, and we do it our own way? God's blessings are connected to our obedience to His instructions. Sometimes we want to figure out the consequences of the next move. We want to be sure that everything fits into our own understanding.

When and how will the breakthrough come?

> *Trust in the Lord with all thine heart; and lean not unto thine own understanding. In all thy ways*

Steps Toward a New Beginning

acknowledge him, and he shall direct thy paths.
Proverbs 3:5-6

He [not you!] shall direct your paths. The "how to" belongs to God. It is our responsibility to hear and obey. We are to position ourselves to hear and obey.

Jesus said, "Launch out into the deep, and let down your nets for a draught." You need to believe in the gifting that God has placed in your life and step out in the pursuit of what God has placed before you.

Isaiah 1:19 says, "If ye be willing and obedient, ye shall eat the good of the land." Instead of fantasizing about the good of the land, ask yourself, "Am I willing and obedient?" The good of the land will be my portion if I am willing and obedient.

Many people would love to have the good of the land, but they are not willing and they are not obedient. They are not willing to do the work that is involved in the process.

Do not despise the day of small beginnings. Does anyone dare despise this day of small beginnings? (Zechariah 4:10 MSG) People want to be overnight successes. You don't go from zero to one thousand. You grow little by little.

Isaiah 60:22 says, "A little one shall become a thousand, and a small one a strong nation." People want to start big, or not start at all. God blesses what you put your hand to.

In Exodus 4:1-2, God said "What do you have in your hand?" The process of growth is crucial to sustaining growth. You need to look for increase in the small things. The blessing is in the details.

Focus on your own business. Develop metrics and things you can look at to measure where you are and where you want to be. I have a weekly measure of what needs to happen in my business.

The Power of a New Beginning

If God is saying that I will fly by the end of the year, I recognize that a plane does not go from the tarmac into the air. It begins to move and moves faster and faster, and then it takes off. The pilot watches the controls.

I must measure where things are right now. I won't just get to the end of the year and take off. I need to move forward a little bit, then move forward a little bit more, before I gain speed.

In Genesis 26:13 (NKJV) God says of Isaac, "The man began to prosper, and continued prospering until he became very prosperous." I have a page in my notebook showing what "prosperous" looks like for me.

If you cannot get through that, you will never go on to "very prosperous." When you get to "began to prosper," you will know three things:

- Where you are
- What you need to start doing
- What you need to stop doing

Sometimes, God is blessing you, but American Express® has become like an employee in your business. I know to the penny how much money is coming into my business. I know how to spend it, but I am still learning to stick closer to the budget.

I remember I had a credit card machine that broke down. I went to another method of scanning credit cards, but the company was still billing me for using the credit card machine. Without watching my monthly expenses closely, I would not have noticed that.

In your "begin to prosper" stage, you begin to look very closely at how much you are spending. When are you transitioning into the "continuing to prosper" stage? It is when you are gaining traction. The plane has started to move. You begin to move away from the tarmac (the stationary place). Things begin to look different. The environment will be different. If you can look out of your window and see people waving, you are not flying yet! You may think you are flying, but you are not.

I began to see a fairly decent balance at the first of each month. Now, I was trying to get away from the tarmac. I needed to gain traction. It was time to cut off all the unnecessary expenses that were taking money out of my pocket.

Recognize unnecessary expenses and limit them. That is discipline. Take note of increase and measure it.

Practice contentment. Start where you are. That is the only place you can start.

People neglect things they can do and focus on things they cannot do. Why? Then, they have an excuse for doing nothing.

I might ask someone, "Have you tried to find a job?"

They might say, "No. I can't, because everything now is on the computer."

That's an excuse to do nothing, instead of doing what they can do.

Second Corinthians 10:12 says, "...measuring themselves by themselves, and comparing themselves among themselves, [they] are not wise." God will always give you enough wisdom and power to do your part.

You need to strike when the iron is hot. My book, *Seize Your Moment (Unmasking Everyday Opportunities),* is available on Amazon. I thought I would be done with it at a certain time, but there was more to be done.

Sometimes, there is a moment of opportunity. You do what must be done within a certain period of time. Amazon gave me a deadline when they were discontinuing editing services. I was to be finished with the book and the companion study guide by that date. I called on others to help with the final edits.

You need to be alert, and aware of what is going on. You need to practice what I call "the turnaround principle."

What is that? This is what I did when I opened my outpatient substance abuse rehab clinic. God said, "Don't look at how big the whole task is from beginning to end. Do your part, and quickly turn the task over to the next person to do the next phase of it."

God will always give you enough wisdom to do your part. The next phase will be done by someone else.

When I opened the rehab, several messages I was listening to were telling me, "Step out!" After listening to preaching for one month, I downloaded the application form. After another month of coming to church, I filled the form out in pencil. After another three months, I placed the form in my "action folder." I would drive back and forth in front of the building where I was supposed to turn it in, but I never went in.

One day, God said, "You need to submit this today." I pulled into the Burger King® parking lot and got the form out of my action folder. I wrote over the pencil in ink, and then I erased the pencil. It should have been typed! I drove to the Orange County Department of Mental Health in Goshen, New York, and submitted it. I said, "This is my application to create a substance abuse clinic in Orange County. Thank you."

About a month later, I received a list of twenty-three or so things I needed to put with the application. Do you know what they did? They assigned me an application number.

The process had started! It was ten times more difficult to fill out and submit the initial application than it was to come up with

Steps Toward a New Beginning

the twenty-three additional things. By submitting the application, I had now become an applicant. That separated me from everyone else. Now the ball was in my court. I needed to put the ball back into their court. One after the other, I submitted the additional things.

Things don't have to be perfect. You don't have to wait until things are perfect! You are better off getting the process started. Even if the application is written in pencil and you have to change it to ink, turn it in. Even if the paperwork is not typed, start the process.

If you look at the transcript I submitted to Amazon, and compare it to the final book product, it is like night and day. They are two completely different things. Do whatever you need to do to get the process started. Many times, we feel paralyzed because our work is not perfect.

That is what I call "the turnaround principle." Do your part and get it over with. Get it back to them. Very often, we have created giants in our heads. Mountains in our imaginations prevent us from stepping out. The Israelites said they were grasshoppers in their own eyes.

When we come upon an opportunity, we immediately think of our own weakness and minimize our strengths. It is important to step out and do it!

Is your name on the application? Is your address on it? Have you completed the required sections? Get it in!

I became someone with a submitted application to start a substance abuse program. The letter they sent back to me said nothing about the application not being typed, or about stray pencil marks. It contained an application number that had been sent to the CEO of the business.

The Power of a New Beginning

It took me two years before I finally opened the program. I did not stop. I did my part each time and sent it back to them. I prayed, "Lord, give me wisdom to do my part."

Do your part. God will do His part. He will bring people around you to do their parts. Everything starts with you doing your part. Then, you will begin to see the fruit of obedience in your life.

Chapter 4

God's Provision for Your New Beginning

In the beginning God created the heaven and the earth. And the earth was without form, and void; and darkness was upon the face of the deep. And the Spirit of God moved upon the face of the waters. And God said, Let there be light. Genesis 1:1-3

There was chaos when God looked at the world. Three key things were there: God's creativity, God's Spirit, and God's spoken Word.

When you begin to look around you at the darkness, the chaos, and the things that are without form and void, recognize that you have access to the same things God had on the inside of Himself. You have His creativity, His Spirit, and the power of His spoken Word.

The Bible talks about how the Spirit of God began to move upon the face of the waters. There are times when you need to allow the Spirit of God and your spirit to move upon the face of the waters in your life.

That is where reflection comes in. You begin to assess. It was when God assessed the situation that He decided the first priority was light. He pictured what He wanted and said, "Let there be light."

Someone may say, "I fell in my room and I have a bruise. I often fall in my room." I ask, "Is there a light in your room?" You can keep treating bruises, but what you really need is a light bulb.

When the Spirit of God begins to move over your situation, He will tell you the order and sequence of things that need to happen in your life.

The Lord showed me exactly what to focus on. He will show you what the first step is in your walk towards creativity.

You have creative ability on the inside. What will you create first?

God could have created man first, but man would have been in the dark. Ask yourself, "Is there light shining on my situation? Can I truly assess what is going on in my life? Where is God leading me? What direction is He giving me?" Psalm 119:130 says, "The entrance of thy words giveth light; it giveth understanding unto the simple."

When the Word of God comes, it automatically shines light on you. Sometimes God may tell you to apologize. You may think, "What did I do? I had a conversation with so-and-so, but I said nothing wrong."

God may say, "It was your attitude. You need to apologize, and to correct your attitude." The Spirit of God will shed light on areas of your life you need to focus on.

You may be telling your problems to everyone around you instead of going directly to God. When a patient comes to me with several complaints, I try to single out one specific thing. What is the one thing that person can do that will begin to make a change in his or her life?

God's Provision for Your New Beginning

God will tell you the first thing you need to do. How often do you have access to light? Twice a year? You need regular access to light. If you are not in the Word of God regularly, if you are not in His presence and fellowshipping with His people, how will you have light? Those things help to give you light.

Guess what? You may have light now, but if you don't meditate on it, you will forget it. If someone calls you and asks what the pastor's message was about Wednesday night, will you know?

The Bible says His mercies are new every morning. (Lam. 3:23) Start life new every day. Each day we are creating our lives. Are you doing it intentionally or by accident? Each day you are creating something.

Are you working out of a blueprint, or are you just seeing how things go? You cannot see the mountain in front of you if you are not going anywhere. If you do not have a destination, you will not know what mountains there are. There may have been mountains you have been fellowshipping with.

Years ago in Nigeria, we didn't have cell phones. People would just drop by on Sunday afternoon and spend the whole day. They didn't have a plan, they were just in the neighborhood, so they dropped by. They would say, "Oh, I was visiting this other person, and I had some time to kill. I thought I would spend it with you."

If you are in school, you may not know how to choose friends. Do you choose them because they are cute? You need a vision of where you are going. Some people can help you get to your destiny. Make friends with those people! You need to recognize what a mountain is. You may already have made friends with the biggest distraction to your destiny.

The Power of a New Beginning

When God wants to increase you, He will introduce you to a person; when the devil wants to decrease you or make you stagnant, he also will introduce you to a person. You need to regularly evaluate who is close to you.

Stop living your life as though it were a rough draft. Some people think that they will be able to come back and correct all their mistakes. They think they will begin to live deliberately when they are forty or fifty years old.

This is real. True life has begun. This is not a test. Your life has begun. Be actively involved in designing your life. Line up with the Creator and find out what He has planned for you.

Begin to make His goals your own goals. Make goals based on God's vision for you. Don't make goals based on how you feel or where you live. Rise above what is going on around you.

Romans 5:17 says, "For if by one man's offence death reigned by one; much more they which receive abundance of grace and of the gift of righteousness shall reign in life by one, Jesus Christ." We need to reign in life by Jesus Christ.

Your gift will make room for you. How does that translate into day-to-day life? Through your gift you will stand before kings; it will create room for you. It will take you out of the regular order and bring you to the front.

What used to take five or ten years will take only a few years. Your gift will bypass the regular order and move you several steps ahead. Your gift will bring you onstage and create something for you.

William Ward says there are three enemies of personal peace: regret over yesterday's mistakes, anxiety over tomorrow's problems, and ingratitude over today's blessings.[1]

God's Provision for Your New Beginning

What are some things that try to prevent our transition to something greater? The first thing is our past. The second thing is fear of failure. The third thing is the present.

God's mercies are new every morning. Your past tries to say, "You have tried this before." That is where the brooding of the Holy Spirit comes in. The Word of God is powerful, sharper than any two-edged sword, and able to pierce asunder the dividing of soul and spirit. (Heb. 4:12)

Many things may be mixed up in our minds, our souls, and our spirits. You may think, "Is this me or is this God?" The Word of God is able to cut through all of that. That is why, as you expose yourself to the Word of God, the Word will let you know what to focus on.

The Bible says the Word is a lamp unto your feet and a light unto your path. (Ps 119:105) A lamp tells you what the next step is. A light tells you the general direction you are moving in.

The Holy Spirit can help you overcome the fear of failure. Why? Christianity is not a self-help enterprise. Before you were created, God had a plan for you. He is trying to get you to accept the plan.

That is the big difference. His plan is a good one. I'm not trying to get you excited for no reason. God's plan is exciting. If your vision does not excite you, you are officially in a rut.

If you are waiting for someone else to give you instructions about your life, you are in trouble. You cannot wait for people to give you direction.

You need to take personal responsibility for your own success. The Holy Spirit can help you deal with the fear of failure. He has a plan for your life, and He can help you overcome fear.

Next, you need to have a vision of where you are going. Proverbs 29:18 says, "Where there is no vision, the people perish." It is all linked in. If you don't have a vision, then everyone can be your friend.

Psalm 90:12 says, "So teach us to number our days, that we may apply our hearts unto wisdom." You need to have vision for your life, and you need to be able to number your days.

When you get older you recognize the value of a year. When you are younger, time seems to go in five-year increments. Older people live year by year. Younger people feel they have unlimited years to fulfill their vision.

As people get older, and reach a certain age, they sometimes get desperate and feel they do not have as much time to fulfill their visions. There are certain milestones that seem to create a sense of desperation in people. Sometimes, older people step out and try to do many things because they feel a sense of desperation.

> The present can be a hindrance if people don't have a vision of where they are going.

A friend of mine who was approaching 50 said she could not wait to get out of the rat race. The present can be a hindrance if people don't have a vision of where they are going. Why? They are consumed with what they are going through right now; they can't even dream of a better future. They are living life day-to-day. Step back and say, "I need a vision for a better future."

Your vision needs to be written down, specific, and motivating. You need to be excited about it. You should read it and say, "Wow! I am going somewhere.

The things I am doing now are all connected to something. I have set myself up so that in two or three years it will all come together. The work I am doing now will all pay off. Completing high school will bring me closer to my goal of college." You need to see each thing you are doing as a step towards your goals.

Seek to excel in school. When you are in elementary school, many awards are given. Some are given for attendance, others for character, and others for achievement. The awards are fewer in middle school. They are even fewer in high school. Once you are done with high school, and you start your journey, the awards are even fewer. There are not as many given in college, and people seldom receive awards at work. We don't just do things to get awards, but I have noticed that those who get awards in school are more likely to be successful. They are more likely to achieve their goals.

You need a written vision for your life. Write the vision down. Expand your mental and spiritual vision. As I said, you cannot know what mountains are before you until you know where you are going.

Do you know where you are going? If not, you won't have to be selective about which road to take.

The extent of your vision is the limit of your possession. You cannot possess what you cannot see. Recognize that the future is bright, and it is yours for the taking.

There is a problem when your eyesight and your vision are the same thing. For you to have a vision, you need knowledge.

I was driving to work and saw several "For Sale" signs in front of some houses. Someone with real estate experience would know which of them would be good investment properties. Getting the knowledge you need is crucial.

The Bible says, where there is life there is hope. (Eccl. 9:4)

The Power of a New Beginning

Some people are so focused on the present. You need to envision where you will be ten years from now.

I got my 30-year mortgage in 2003. I signed a contract for 30 years; I refinanced it later for 15 years. I told my wife that I should have signed a 15-year mortgage in the first place. It would have been worthwhile, even though discipline would have been required to set aside enough money each month to make the payments. If so, I could have celebrated my mortgage-burning ceremony in 2018.

Getting wisdom from God is so important for your life. Where do you see yourself in ten years?

Satan was willing to kill Jesus at two years of age because he saw Jesus' potential. The most effective time for the enemy to get to you is when you are small. You are most vulnerable then. That is why the fetus stays in the mother's womb until it can survive outside. When it is small it is vulnerable.

You will have ideas, and the enemy will try to snatch them and say, "This is not a big deal." No! Don't despise the days of small beginnings. You need to realize that, although you are dealing with something small right now, it has the potential to be very, very great.

Don't just tell your plans to anyone. Zacharias was unable to speak because he started saying the wrong things. You are better off saying nothing than saying the wrong things.

> *Now in the sixth month, the angel Gabriel was sent from God to a city of Galilee, named Nazareth, to a virgin pledged to be married to a man whose name was Joseph, of David's house. The virgin's name was Mary. Having come in, the angel said to her, "Rejoice, you highly favored one! The Lord is with you. Blessed are you among women!" But when she*

God's Provision for Your New Beginning

> *saw him, she was greatly troubled at the saying, and considered what kind of salutation this might be. The angel said to her, "Don't be afraid, Mary, for you have found favor with God.* Luke 1:26-29 WEB

What happens when a big God gives you a ridiculous promise? There are times when a big God gives you big promises. This is not ridiculous to Him because He is bigger than the promise He has given you.

> *Behold, you will conceive in your womb, and give birth to a son, and will call his name 'Jesus.' He will be great, and will be called the Son of the Most High. The Lord God will give him the throne of his father, David, and he will reign over the house of Jacob forever. There will be no end to his Kingdom." Mary said to the angel, "How can this be, seeing I am a virgin?" The angel answered her, "The Holy Spirit will come on you, and the power of the Most High will overshadow you. Therefore also the holy one who is born from you will be called the Son of God. Behold, Elizabeth, your relative, also has conceived a son in her old age; and this is the sixth month with her who was called barren. For nothing spoken by God is impossible." Mary said, "Behold, the servant of the Lord; let it be done to me according to your word."* Luke 1:31-38

Even though God's promise seems so far-fetched, we need to have the attitude of Mary: "Let it be done to me according to your word." Line up the vision of your life with what God has in store for you.

The Power of a New Beginning

Don't create a vision based on your past. Don't create a vision based on your fears. Don't create a vision based on your present. Don't even create a vision that is just a little bit better than where you are.

We need to say, "Let it be done to me according to your word," and then be obedient to whatever God has instructed you to do.

Initiate something and stop living just for today. Give God something to multiply.

A seed may be in the form of your getting an education, giving of money, giving of your time by volunteering, or investing. You need to sow something so you can reap something. If you don't sow anything you don't reap anything.

There *is* a limit to how much God can bless you; it is based on what you are doing now.

I remember when I was working for someone else. I looked at the amount they were paying me, and I said, "The zeros at the end of this number need to be increased." I needed a raise! Everyone else in the business would have to be increased first, and then I would receive more. That is why a raise is usually only 1, 2 or 3 percent.

You may be giving tithe and believing for increase, but you also need to have something on the side that doesn't have to pass through anyone else to get to you. It doesn't have to go to A, B, or C, it comes straight to U! The blessing goes straight into your bank account. That is direct deposit!

What is the most God can bless me based on what I am doing now? Genesis 39:2 says that God made all Joseph did to prosper. All! All that Joseph did!

No matter what your gift is, you don't have to do nine or ten different things. I am a psychiatrist. I charge a certain rate for patients depending on the setting. If God wants to prosper all I do, I have to be willing to do more than one thing or be open to doing the same thing in different settings.

There are settings where my work is administrative, and there are settings where my work is direct patient care. That is what I have been given to work with. You have to work with the gift God has given you.

> *The Lord shall cause thine enemies that rise up against thee to be smitten before thy face: they shall come out against thee one way, and flee before thee seven ways. The Lord shall command the blessing upon thee in thy storehouses, and in all that thou settest thine hand unto; and he shall bless thee in the land which the Lord thy God giveth thee.*
> Deuteronomy 28:7-8

Sometimes we don't step out because we see the hindrances. God opened my eyes to this scripture. It says, "The Lord shall cause thine enemies that rise up against thee to be smitten before thy face." For your enemy to be defeated, it needs to be before your face. The enemy will not be defeated if you are on your bed. That means you must stand up and walk to your enemy.

Which enemy have you decided to walk towards? People want God to defeat the enemy before they even get up, but the Lord will defeat your enemy before your face.

The Red Sea was not parted until they walked up to it.

You need to walk towards your promise, irrespective of what enemy is there. God's promise is to remove your enemy when you get there. We say, "God, as soon as you remove that enemy, I will take a shower."

The Power of a New Beginning

God says, "Take a shower. Get dressed. Go for that interview. Stand before the CEO, and I will defeat them before your face." You need to be looking at them face-to-face.

God has given you more than you are willing to take. Isaiah 60:1 says, "Arise, shine; for thy light is come, and the glory of the Lord is risen upon thee."

What are you going to do with the light? God wants you to keep walking, and He will remove the next hindrance. It is not really a hindrance unless you are walking.

Some of us have a lot of hindrances in our minds. For those of us who have taken the steps, we know that God is parting the Red Sea. He gives us wisdom on demand! The lazy man wants assurance before he leaves his bed that everything will be okay.

You don't need God's wisdom when you are on your bed or when you are on Facebook whiling away the time. You need God's wisdom when you are making a proposal to a CEO explaining the idea for a business venture you worked on between 6 PM and 8 PM each night after work.

When the CEO asks you why he should invest in your idea, God's wisdom will come up inside you. You may have jotted down twenty hindrances why you won't get funding, but hindrances will not prevail. God's promise is that He will remove the next hindrance. He won't start with the fifth one, but the first one. When you get past that one, He will remove the next one.

He removes hindrances as you go forward. He will not give you seven green lights in a row. When I am driving, I want to see several green lights ahead of me; but, I can only go through one green light at a time. One!

I have found out that the biggest hindrance is not the giant, it is the lack of desire. Not wanting to arise, complacency, inertia, lack of motivation, insufficient drive, mediocrity, status quo, comfort zone, or leaving well enough alone. Call it what you may, but lack of desire is the biggest hindrance.

We need to arise first, before we can shine.

Your part is to arise, God will make you shine.

Arising means obedience to God's Word, it means doing your part. It means enrolling in that course, filling out that application, registering that small business, getting a lease for that store front, or signing up for that side job. It is doing whatever your hand finds to do. It is taking a step toward your destiny.

Chapter 5

The Power of Self-Discipline

We are going to discuss the power of self-discipline. Self-discipline is important because it produces the patterns of behavior or specific actions in your daily life that are required for your success. In short, discipline is what you need to get you to where you want to go.

Dictionary.com says discipline is "behavior in accord with rules of conduct, behavior and order maintained by training and control."[1]

A colleague said, "Self-discipline is what you say yes to. Self-control is what you say no to." Self-control is a fruit of the spirit. We see that in Galatians 5:22-23.

Second Timothy 1:7 is a scripture we quote often, but do not think of in reference to self-control.

> *For God did not give us a spirit of timidity (of cowardice, of craven and cringing and fawning fear), but [He has given us a spirit] of power and of love and of calm and well-balanced mind and discipline and self-control. Second Timothy 1:7 (AMPC)*

The Power of a New Beginning

This is the kind of mind God has given us. Any task worth doing will require self-discipline.

The disciples were called "disciples" because they disciplined themselves after the lifestyle and teachings of Jesus. Believers are called to reach out to the lost, and also to make disciples. We are to teach people to discipline themselves after the teachings of Christ.

That doesn't come by hearing a message once. God wants us to be disciples. Being a disciple is not a title. It is not the same as being the member of a church.

Self-discipline gives you staying power. It helps you set realistic goals in a reasonable time frame. If your goal does not require you to be self-disciplined, you have not stretched yourself. We are required to be disciplined.

For example, one of the things we will have to do consistently is meditate on the Word of God. Often, people don't do that because they lack discipline. We all may want to do it, but some have not prioritized it enough.

In order to establish this important discipline in the Word of God, we need to know why this discipline is so vital. We need to have faith that our time in the Word brings light to our path and strength to our spirit.

When we believe that we are to desire the sincere milk of the Word that we may grow thereby (First Peter 2:2) and that the Word of grace is able to build us up and give us an inheritance (Acts 20:32), it begins to direct our decisions and behavior. Our faith in what we are doing provides a momentum.

As we develop ourselves in self-discipline, another important part of the process is to set goals for ourselves that will challenge and motivate us.

The Power of Self-Discipline

Avoid setting goals that are unrealistic. We all have dreams and ambitions. We have the ability to overcome challenges we face. Most goals are not achieved because we underestimate the challenges involved or fail to factor them in.

For instance, it is easy to say, "I want to lose weight," but that means you will have to give up some things. You will have to wake up earlier and spend less time watching TV. We underestimate the amount of time it will take.

When you discipline yourself, you find time you didn't know you had.

When I was writing my first book, I kept searching for a serene place to write. Then, I realized that the hour before work is probably my most productive time. I didn't need to go to the beach; I only needed to go as far as the computer. Most of my book was written during the early morning hours. I felt very inspired during that time.

One great benefit in developing yourself in discipline is to identify and clarify your priorities. This will enable you to take the right course of action and achieve the right results.

One example could be that you want to be more disciplined in spending. If so, take control over purchases. Choose in advance what you are going to buy, how much you are going to spend, or what your budget for that project will be.

Some people have self-control over large purchases, but not with small ones. Some people have self-control over small purchases, but not with large ones.

Do you spend $5.00 a day, or do you make your own coffee? The man who makes his own coffee in order to save money may want to take a $10,000 vacation.

Everyone has a weak spot. Couples need to help each other balance these weaknesses out. If you are single, you will have to find your own balance.

Life is in phases. You need to know what phase you are in. Are you in the reaping phase or the sowing phase? When it comes to giving, you need to know what phase you are in.

Do you give your tithe? When you give over and above your tithe, you are giving offerings. You can't tithe one week, and the next week use your tithe money to pay a bill. Plan your giving. Give ten percent of your income. Be strategic. You can't just give a big amount when you receive your tax refund. Plan your giving!

Maintaining your focus on the priority will help you stay the course. You can easily become persistent in your actions toward the end results.

Persistence allows people to claim great accomplishments. Michael Jordan was turned down by his high school basketball coach. When he asked what he needed to do to get on the team, he was told to master the basics. He practiced his shooting, his dribbling, and his passing. The rest is history. Persistence will get you further than raw talent.

You need to create your own inspiration that will be a reliable source of encouragement in difficult times. Don't depend on others for motivation. Learn to motivate yourself. Learn how to encourage yourself in the Lord.

> *But also for this very reason, giving all diligence, add to your faith virtue, to virtue knowledge, to knowledge self-control, to self-control perseverance, to perseverance godliness, to godliness brotherly kindness, and to brotherly kindness love. For if these things are yours and abound, you will be neither barren nor unfruitful in*

The Power of Self-Discipline

the knowledge of our Lord Jesus Christ. Second Peter 1:5-8 NKJV

Sometimes we are unfruitful because there are certain things we have not added to our faith. It says you should add these things to your faith so that you will not be unfruitful or barren, failing to bear fruit. It is a bit like a recipe. If you don't do things in order, or you leave something out, you will not have the desired results.

Add to your faith virtue, and to your virtue knowledge. You need self-control and perseverance. You need to add these things to your faith. What does that mean? Two people may have faith, but only one of them has these other things. Only one of them will be fruitful.

For he who lacks these things is shortsighted, even to blindness, and has forgotten that he was cleansed from his old sins. Second Peter 1:9 NKJV

The Bible says, "...add to your faith virtue, to virtue knowledge, to knowledge self-control, to self-control perseverance, to perseverance godliness, to godliness brotherly kindness, and to brotherly kindness love." If you lack these things you will be barren and unfruitful.

It means you have forgotten what God has done for you. He has cleansed you from your old sins. Getting saved and receiving faith is not enough. You need these other things. That is where discipleship comes in.

These are not things people get excited about. Most people are not interested in developing self-control. Anyone who has accomplished anything will tell you about perseverance. People think just because God has given them instructions on how to start a project, that they don't need to exert themselves or use discipline.

God knows more than anyone what you are capable of. You can tell the doctor or your friend, "That is too hard." You cannot tell God that. He knows that if you want it badly enough you will do it. God will not tell you to do more than you are able to do.

Once discipline is in your system, it becomes a natural part of you. This is important because if you have discipline you have everything. Proverbs 16:32 says he that controls his spirit is better than he that takes a city.

When you base your life on principles, 99% of your decisions are already made. You won't say, "We'll see how it goes."

When it comes to making friends, principle will rule out certain people. You are disciplined. You know where you are headed. You won't look for a quick break. Purpose does what it must; talent does what it can.[3]

Whatever God has asked you to do, it will require discipline. It will require more than getting a word from God, getting excited, and running around. Don't be one of those who end the year the same way they began it.

Chapter 6

The Greater One Is in You.

Next, we will discuss the fact that the Greater One is in you. Ed Cole says there are three levels of knowledge: God is for me, God is with me, God is in me.[1] I will add that this is also true of love.

Psalm 56:9 says, "When I cry unto thee, then shall mine enemies turn back: this I know; for God is for me." Accept only those thoughts that line up with God's Word and His will for your life, and that contribute to your success.

GOD IS FOR ME

What does that mean? When you have a conviction that God is for you, you recognize that you have hope. You have the power to start again. You know you can overcome disappointment. It helps with self-esteem. Whatever your failings are, you know God has forgiven you and you are now His child. You know you can overcome situations you face. This is the first level of conviction of the love of God. Do you believe God is for you?

GOD IS WITH ME

What does that mean? You have peace and security. It gives you comfort no matter what situation you find yourself in. It lets you know He is with you always, not just in church. When you walk through the valley of the shadow of death His rod and staff comfort you. It helps you overcome adversity and face danger.

This is the second level of conviction of the love of God, but it is the highest level in which man could operate in the Old Testament. God is for me and God is with me. That is as far as people could go before Jesus came on the scene.

GOD IS IN ME

This causes you to dream beyond your greatest imaginations. You see things, not as they are, but as God sees them. "God is in me" conviction helps you know you have the same authority Jesus had. It gives you the creative power to reshape your destiny.

You go to a store to exchange something. Sometimes the people authorize an exchange; sometimes they must ask the supervisor to do it. If the supervisor lacks the authority, he or she may have to call upon the store manager. You must go through several levels.

In certain situations, you may feel that you need to call your pastor or call a friend to pray for you. It depends on your conviction of the love of God.

When you begin to know God is in you, it is like having the store manager inside. You have permission to authorize whatever it is because you are operating in the name of Jesus.

> *Verily I say unto you, Whatsoever ye shall bind on earth shall be bound in heaven: and whatsoever ye*

The Greater One Is in You

> *shall loose on earth shall be loosed in heaven.*
> Matthew 18:18

You don't need to check and see what God thinks. You don't need to see if God wants you to get healed or if He is trying to teach you something. You don't need to see if God wants you to be depressed. You don't even have to go that route.

If you wake up, and you are feeling down, you say, "God is in me; we are going to take care of this right now. We are not waiting. We are not going through the same pattern. The Greater One lives inside me; His name is Jesus." First John 4:4 says, "...greater is he that is in you, than he that is in the world."

You don't just have access to power somewhere in heaven. The power is resident and charged up. You don't need to call for backup. Backup is already there. You have your own strength, but your backup generator is automatic. The Holy Ghost is already there.

You have the mind of God concerning situations. Depression is not right. Being broke is not right. I don't try to figure out "why God did this to me." This is of the devil. I rebuke it in the name of Jesus. God is in me. That is another level of conviction. I have the power to make a change.

I don't have to consult with the Power Giver. I already did before I left the house. I already know His will and His purpose for my life. Anything inconsistent with it has to go. Luke 10:19 says, "Behold, I give unto you power...over all the power of the enemy."

You are seated together with Christ in heavenly places. You understand authority and you understand position. You already have Someone living inside you Who can take care of the situation. You don't need permission. You are licensed to carry

The Power of a New Beginning

your spiritual weapon. You don't need to go for training each time a situation comes up. You are ready to discharge it on demand.

When the thief breaks in, do you go for more training, or do you press the button? Ephesians 6:13 says, "…having done all [to stand], stand." Put on the whole armor of God so you can withstand all the wiles of the enemy (Eph. 6:11). You put on the whole armor of God; the enemy is upset when you come on the scene.

God is in you. You look beyond your situation. You bring heaven on the scene.

It is not just about you, it is about being positioned to be a blessing. It is about helping someone who needs a release of joy, a release of peace, and a release of the power you carry. It is not a matter of getting people to prop you up so you can feel happy every day. It is like a live wire is operating on the inside of you.

God gives you revelation before the problem comes. Jesus was never puzzled when they asked Him a question. He was prepared. He knew what He was going to say in every situation. He gives you access to the same power that was at work when Jesus rose from the dead.

> *He that spared not his own Son, but delivered him up for us all, how shall he not with him also freely give us all things?* Romans 8:32

God caused His Son to die on the cross and then raised Him up; how can we worry whether or not he will meet our needs? Darkness, ignorance, or both will keep you from walking in resurrection power.

You don't need resurrection power to live a life of mediocrity. Resurrection power is to put you over. First John 5:4 says, "For whatsoever is born of God overcometh the world…" Either you have forgotten Who you are born of, or you have overestimated the power of the world. This is the power, not just to overcome problems, but to walk in newness of life.

> *Therefore we are buried with him by baptism into death: that like as Christ was raised up from the dead by the glory of the Father, even so we also should walk in newness of life.* Romans 6:4

Somebody posted this on Facebook: "Overcoming death by death." What does that mean? It means you overcome death by means of Jesus' death. That's what the Bible says.

> *And deliver them who through fear of death were all their lifetime subject to bondage.* Hebrews 2:15

Jesus' death is there to help you overcome the fear of death. The most powerful thing you can use to overcome death is death. Not yours, but the death that was done for your sake. That is the boldness we have. We have died. We have been buried with Him. We walk in newness of life.

> *I am crucified with Christ: nevertheless I live; yet not I, but Christ liveth in me: and the life which I now live in the flesh I live by the faith of the Son of God, who loved me, and gave himself for me. I do not frustrate the grace of God: for if righteousness comes by the law, then Christ is dead in vain.* Galatians 2:20-21

If we know this, and death comes, we can say, "I have died already. The life I am living now is the life of Christ. Unless you have enough power to incapacitate Christ you can't incapacitate me."

We know that perfect love casts out fear.

The Power of a New Beginning

There is no fear in love; but perfect love casteth out fear: because fear hath torment. He that feareth is not made perfect in love. First John 4:18

If you are living like a disciple, crucifying your flesh, asking God for more of Him, allowing the new life to walk on the inside of you, the fear of death is not there. You have gone through the death process already. First Corinthians 15:31 says, "I die daily."

You don't die physically each day, but you need to crucify certain things in your flesh daily. You should have a habit of dying. You should say, "Christ, this is not like You. Take it away." The fear of death should not be a problem for us. We have been crucified with Christ. It is no longer I who live.

The fear of death is the most powerful fear there is. The Bible uses extremes. We can now come back to the little fears that bother you like the fear of spiders, the fear of going broke, or the fear of unemployment. If God can deliver you from the fear of death, He can deliver you from all fear. Every fear is a bit of death. Anything, if magnified, that leads to the fear of death is a bit of death.

> When you fully identify with Christ, you live a life of boldness.

God is not just trying to take away your problems and your burdens. God is trying to change your life. He wants you to put down the old one and take up the new one. God wants you to walk in newness of life.

When you fully identify with Christ, you live a life of boldness. I cannot go where Christ would not go.

God is not trying to renovate your life. He is trying to take the old you out. That means He wants to kill the old you, so you can identify with Christ and walk in newness of life.

The Greater One Is in You

> *Therefore if any man be in Christ, he is a new creature: old things are passed away; behold, all things are become new.* Second Corinthians 5:17

God wants old things to pass away and all things to become new. He wants your righteousness to be new, your perspective to be new, and your mind to be renewed.

He doesn't want to make a prosperous sinner. He wants the life of God to be lived out in you. He wants you to live the life of faith of Jesus Christ, and He wants that faith to work itself out in the day-to-day situations of life, in your relationships, and in the way you see yourself.

God in you is a different level of conviction. It lets you know that God is able to do exceedingly abundantly above all that we ask or think, according to the power that worketh in us (Eph. 3:20). You are a live wire!

First John 4:17 says "...as he is, so are we in this world." There is no delay. This is happening in real time. We don't have to wait. What you bind on earth is bound in heaven.

You are called to operate in the highest conviction of God's love in the New Testament.

> *God [in His eternal plan] chose to make known to them how great for the Gentiles are the riches of the glory of this mystery, which is Christ in and among you, the hope and guarantee of [realizing the] glory. We proclaim Him, warning and instructing everyone in all wisdom [that is, with comprehensive insight into the word and purposes of God], so that we may present every person complete in Christ [mature, fully trained, and perfect in Him—the Anointed].* Colossians 1:27-28 AMP

The Power of a New Beginning

The hope of any man on this earth is Christ. No matter how wayward he is, if you can introduce him to Christ, the process of glory has begun. You never know what God has in store or what glory will come out of that life. No negative condition can be permanent if Christ is in it.

Second Corinthians 2:18 tells us not to look at the things that are temporal, but at what is eternal. Get comfortable with "greater." Greater is in you.

When you are in Christ, the Greater One is in you. No matter what problems you face, the Greater One is in you. Can't reach your best friend so he can pray for you? The Greater One is in you.

> *Beloved, let us love one another, for love is of God; and everyone who loves is born of God and knows God. He who does not love does not know God, for God is love. In this the love of God was manifested toward us, that God has sent His only begotten Son into the world, that we might live through Him.* First John 4:7-9

It doesn't say He came to solve our problems or to make our life a little better. He came that we might live through Him. That is the love of God because none of us deserve it. You ask for bread; God has put you on the throne.

> *In this is love, not that we loved God, but that He loved us and sent His Son to be the propitiation for our sins. Beloved, if God so loved us, we also ought to love one another.* First John 4:10-11

The Bible recognizes that we don't start off this way. We have to be perfected. Another word for *perfect* is "mature."

The Greater One Is in You

> *Love has been perfected among us in this: that we may have boldness in the day of judgment; because as He is, so are we in this world.* First John 4:17

You start off knowing God is for you. You come to know that God is with you. Finally, you get to the level of knowing God is in you. When God comes to judge you, you know you haven't spent your life just asking for things. You have spent your life living His life. As He is, so are we in this world. There is no fear in love, but perfect love casts out all fear.

Yes, you can take authority over the enemy and cast down imaginations. Ultimately, you need to pray for a revelation of the love of God. Fear has torment. He who fears has not been made perfect in love.

First John 4:19 says, "We love Him because He first loved us."

> *I can do all things [which He has called me to do] through Him who strengthens and empowers me [to fulfill His purpose—I am self-sufficient in Christ's sufficiency; I am ready for anything and equal to anything through Him who infuses me with inner strength and confident peace.]* Philippians 4:13 AMP

You have a live wire inside you. You are equal to anything because He infuses you with inner strength and confident peace that will make you able to accomplish and overcome anything in life. Romans 8:37 says, "Yet in all these things we are more than conquerors through Him who loved us."

Chapter 7

Take Control of Your Destiny

For I know the thoughts that I think toward you, says the Lord, thoughts of peace and not of evil, to give you a future and a hope. Jeremiah 29:11 NKJV

My question to you is this: is there a difference between how you see yourself and where you find yourself? That is what we are going to address in this chapter.

Student, do you feel that you are an intelligent person, but it is not reflected in your grades?

Employee, do you feel that you have missed too many promotions? Do you feel stuck below your potential?

Are you in a relationship you know is not right for you, but you have concluded it is better than nothing?

Are you putting up with someone who is not treating you right, but you are afraid of being alone?

Is there a difference between how you see yourself and where you find yourself?

The Power of a New Beginning

You may have a desire to branch out, perhaps to create your own business, but fear is holding you back.

You may have a desire to return to college, but you have allowed time and the concerns of daily life to steal your motivation.

You may be a retiree on a fixed income, and you know your creativity is worth more than your monthly Social Security check. You used to be a happy person, but you have delegated your happiness to someone else.

Do you sense there is more to life than you are currently experiencing?

Herbert Prochnow said, "There is a time when we must firmly choose the course which we will follow, or the endless drift of events will make the decision for us."[1]

Are you living or are you drifting? God woke me up several years ago and said, "Somebody, somewhere is planning your future." Whether you acknowledge it or not, this is so.

I was in a meeting with our vice president the other day, and she said there was a new opportunity opening up to run for the ACT Team. ACT stands for Assertive Community Treatment. It is a program which helps people with severe mental illness who are not able to get to the clinic. Psychiatrists and an entire treatment team go to them.

I said, "I know we are pretty busy now, so we are not going to apply for it."

She said, "Why not? We are already applying for it."

Whether I knew it or not, the application was going in. My name was there as the Medical Director overseeing the program. Someone was planning my life even before I knew what was going on. She sent me a text later explaining that we had been approved for the first stage and were sure to get the contract. So, while I am still becoming familiar with the seven clinical sites I am supervising, they just added another responsibility.

Somebody is planning your life for you. It may be a boss, whether he or she likes you or not. It may be a boyfriend with ulterior motives. It may be a union leader charmed by politicians. Somebody somewhere is planning your life for you. That's why you need to be actively involved in the course of your life.

Psalm 66:12 says "You have caused men to ride over our heads; We went through fire and through water; But You brought us out to rich *fulfillment."* (NKJV) God has brought us to a place of rich fulfillment. He wants us to experience rich fulfillment.

Anything other than that is below what God has in store for us.

We see some keys from the scriptures. Luke 15 contains a description of someone who saw a difference between who he was, and where he found himself. The story of the prodigal son is one that many of us already know.

> *Then He said: "A certain man had two sons. And the younger of them said to his father, 'Father, give me the portion of goods that falls to me.' So he divided to them his livelihood. And not many days after, the younger son gathered all together, journeyed to a far country, and there wasted his possessions with prodigal living. But when he had spent all, there arose a severe famine in that land, and he began to be in want. Then he went and joined himself to a citizen of that country, and he sent him into his fields to feed swine. And he would gladly have filled his stomach with the pods that the swine ate, and no one gave him anything.*

The Power of a New Beginning

"But when he came to himself, he said, 'How many of my father's hired servants have bread enough and to spare, and I perish with hunger! I will arise and go to my father, and will say to him, "Father, I have sinned against heaven and before you, and I am no longer worthy to be called your son. Make me like one of your hired servants.'

"And he arose and came to his father. But when he was still a great way off, his father saw him and had compassion, and ran and fell on his neck and kissed him. And the son said to him, 'Father, I have sinned against heaven and in your sight, and am no longer worthy to be called your son.'

"But the father said to his servants, 'Bring out the best robe and put it on him, and put a ring on his hand and sandals on his feet. And bring the fatted calf here and kill it, and let us eat and be merry; for this my son was dead and is alive again; he was lost and is found.' And they began to be merry. Luke 15:11-24 (NKJV)

The first thing we see here is awareness. Awareness led to what I would call the right question. He said to himself, "How many of my father's hired servants have bread enough and to spare, and I perish with hunger!"

You cannot ask yourself the right question until you come to yourself. No one can come to yourself for you. You must ask yourself some key questions. Are you living at your full potential? When you look around, what do you see? Coming to yourself has to do with taking a step back and looking at your situation, your business, your relationships, and saying, "What is going on here?"

Take Control of Your Destiny

In this case, hunger, desolation, isolation, and desperation made him reflect on his situation. He became aware of the pigs. He became aware also of a relationship he had ignored.

We need to be aware of relationships we may have ignored.

Some people allow their pride to get in the way. Instead of feeding pigs, they decide to milk cows.

He knew he needed to get out of the animal kingdom and get back to a relationship. He knew his problem was not livestock; his problem was a relationship. He said, "Even my father's servants have more than enough." He became aware that there was something he could do about his situation.

He knew that there was a relationship which, once restored, could change his standard of living.

Which relationship in your life needs to be restored? Is it a relationship with God? With a man of God?

He retraced his steps. He did not blame anyone. He did not blame his friends who blew the money with him. He did not blame a political party, the neighborhood, or even his spouse.

You need to remove distractions in order to become aware. Some people are too busy feeding pigs to know that it doesn't have to be that way.

You don't have to be in a rut to be aware. Meditating on the Word of God will bring awareness to you of who you are in Christ. You can come to yourself through crisis, through revelation, or through counsel. Good counsel can help you see where you are and help you come to yourself.

You don't have to be in a crisis. Revelation from the Word of God can help you come to yourself. We need to remove distractions and choose the good part, as Mary did.

The Power of a New Beginning

In Luke 10:38-42 Martha was distracted, but Mary sat at Jesus' feet and listened to Him. You don't have to be in a crisis to receive revelation and counsel.

God can plant a question in your heart that is designed to begin the process of change.

Sometimes God's direction does not come in the way you anticipate. It may just come in the form of a question. The three lepers in Second Kings asked, "Why are we sitting here until we die?"

The previous job I had at West Point was a comfortable position. I had advanced from the role of consultant to that of full-time employee. I was receiving federal benefits. I was a consultant for six years, and a full-time employee for two years.

I began to sense there was something more God wanted me to do. A position came open for medical director, and it paid significantly more than I was getting, but the responsibility was much greater. I looked over the application online. I knew the place, and the problems there. I would be supervising eight or nine doctors. There were eight different sites over two counties, including a hospital.

I wondered whether or not I was ready. The word came up in my spirit, "Why sit here until we die?" That was it. An angel didn't come from heaven to tell me to fill out the application. It just came in the form of a question: "Why sit here until we die?"

That was it! A word came at church that day about stepping out and doing what God tells you to do. That word had already been stirring in my heart. "Why sit here until we die?" I could not let go of that word.

Take Control of Your Destiny

When God plants a question in your heart, it is meant to lead to something. Jesus asked many questions. I decided to apply for the position and was offered it before the end of the week.

The next thing the prodigal son did is interesting. He came up with the right evaluation and it led to what I would call a holy discontent. He realized there was a significant difference between how he saw himself and where he found himself. He refused to be satisfied with the status quo. He refused to leave things the way they were.

Sometimes you have to have a holy discontent. Some people may call it pride, but you know when you are operating way below your abilities.

You may think, "This is good enough. It is well above average." The person he went to when he asked for the job feeding pigs did not know about his inheritance. He did not know where he came from. No matter how well your boss knows you, your boss does not know your full potential.

That's why I choose not to worry about work after 5 PM. They pay me to work from 9 AM to 5 PM. From 5 PM to 9 AM I am working for myself. My creativity does not end at 4:30 PM. For some people, it shuts down. They can't think anymore. My second wind kicks in about 3:00 PM. You need to have a holy discontent.

The prodigal son thought to himself, "I am operating below my natural heritage." He didn't even consider the spiritual one. He just thought about how his father's servants were living.

If you come from a good family, why do you put up with an abusive relationship? Get up! Your parents raised you well. Not everyone came from an abusive home. Sometimes you have to say, "Where am I coming from?" Even if you came from an abusive home, you should still want better for yourself.

The prodigal son did not need a revelation from above; he remembered his natural heritage and said, "I can do better than this."

He knew he had squandered his inheritance, so he was not going to try to get a second one. He just said, "Listen, even the servants are doing better. I want a servant's job. That is better than feeding pigs."

Some people would rather feed pigs than work at McDonalds, because if they work at McDonalds other people will see them. You would be amazed if you knew the jobs people choose so that no one will see them.

He was not sure the father would restore him. He had blown his inheritance. Don't forget that! We read the story knowing the outcome. All he wanted was a job as a servant.

People would be coming to the house seeing him living in the servants' quarters while his brother was living in the main house. He was prepared to do that because he was tired of feeding pigs. Because of pride, some people would rather feed the pigs.

Guess what? He figured that after the first time he encountered his father's friends, and they saw that he was a servant, it would be old news. It wouldn't be a surprise. They would say, "This used to be a son, now he is a servant." Get over it. At least he is not feeding pigs. Even Pharaoh wanted more time with the frogs. How many more days with pigs or frogs do you need?

Some people are even too prideful to feed their own bellies. They don't want to feed pigs; they don't want to milk cows; they don't want to work at McDonalds. They just want someone to take care of them. They want a nice church lady with a good job. She has a 401K, a nice car, and some property. Why go to work?

Take Control of Your Destiny

Perhaps they would pray, "Lord, please give me one of those ladies from the church who has been focused on the Word for the last twenty years, waiting for a breakthrough. I want to be someone's breakthrough, Lord Jesus!"

She would say, "You need to get your own breakthrough. You don't know how long it has taken me to get where I am. I am not going to waste it on a prodigal."

God does not always need to change your circumstances. Sometimes He needs to give you a holy discontent. That will lead to a shift. You may have been comfortable in your circumstances for twenty years. All God needs to do is drop a question into your mind. It is a holy discontent.

You have been in the same relationship for a long time, not going anywhere. The guy is making promises but treating you with disdain. You wake up one day and say, "Why?" People in Nigeria jokingly used to call it "Kwhy?"

You look around. Pigs looked good to you yesterday, but you wake up one morning and ask, "What am I doing with pigs?"

A guy does not go from living in his father's inheritance to feeding pigs in one day. It is a gradual process. He didn't take the job by accident. He knew there were pigs.

He had lost some stuff, but he still had his posse hanging around: Augustus, Julius, Shaquita, Joe, and the guy who held the money bag when they went to a club to rap. He had a Facebook page; he was on Instagram. Everything was going well.

Then, the next month Augustus left. Shaquita left. Everyone left except Joe. Joe said, "No matter what, I am with you. I am not here for the money." After two months of not getting anything to eat, Joe said, "It's not you; it's me. My grandmother died. I've got to go, but I'll be back."

The Power of a New Beginning

By the time someone decides to get a job feeding pigs, he has come a long way. It wasn't a one-day thing. It was a gradual process. Now, no one wants to give him anything. Then, he thought the pigs' food looked good. He looked around and thought, "What am I doing here?"

> If you wait for others to evaluate your life for you, you are officially in trouble.

You need to evaluate yourself. You need to evaluate relationships. If you wait for others to evaluate your life for you, you are officially in trouble. Evaluate where you want to be as well as where you are. You must know where you are.

If you feel like you are in the sky, but you look out the window and see pigs, you are not flying. If you look at your checkbook, and the balance is not where you want to be, you need to make some changes.

David Oyedepo of Nigeria says, "Life is in stages and men are in sizes."[2] He is talking about where you are in life, your financial state, and things you should be going after.

When you are in an apartment and living as if you are in a dream house, you are attempting to operate in the wrong stage. When you are meant to be in school, but you are spending your time doing other things, you are attempting to operate in the wrong stage.

"Life is in stages and men are in sizes." People always want to be in the reaping phase, but they don't know there is a sowing phase. Everybody wants to be in the "living large" phase. You need to know what stage you are in.

> *To everything there is a season, A time for every purpose under heaven.* Ecclesiastes 3:1

Take Control of Your Destiny

You need to invest in your education and not in debt. You need to invest in knowledge and not in sneakers. You need to invest in the Word of God and not in fairy tales. You need people around you that will speak into your life.

The older you get the more difficult it becomes to find people who will speak into your life. That is why I treasure my wife so much. She is not afraid to speak the truth. Sometimes the truth hurts, though.

I recently spoke to someone in recovery. He has embraced spirituality and was elevating himself to a new level. His wife said, "I am happy you are no longer using drugs, but I am sad you are on a new level I don't think I can achieve."

He said, "My wife has put me on a pedestal."

I said, "You are in trouble." Then, I told him something I had never said to anyone before: "On her worst day, your wife has something to add to you on your best day." Never make your wife feel you are on some kind of pedestal. He received it and shared it with his wife.

If everyone has placed you on a pedestal, you are in trouble. You need people who will tell you the truth, so you can evaluate where you are. The older you get, the harder they are to find.

Young people say, "Why are you getting into my business?" Trust me, when you get older, you'll want someone to get into your business.

Some people just want to watch you self-destruct. You are headed down to jail, and someone says, "His sneakers are still good, and he has a nice haircut." Examine yourself. Test yourself.

> *Examine yourselves as to whether you are in the faith.* Second Corinthians 13:5

Next, the prodigal son made a decision. He came to the right conclusion. He decided to arise and go to his father. He realized that one bad decision need not lead to a lifetime of bad decisions.

Someone said, "I left that church. I left that pastor." Did they say you couldn't come back? "I left that pastor." One bad decision need not lead to a lifestyle of bad decisions.

He knew it was not too late to change his mind. When you have evaluated, what will your conclusion be? A decision means letting go of other options and narrowing it down to one.

You ask someone, "Have you found a job?"

They say, "I'm so glad you asked. I applied, but the complexity of the application has led to a phased approach for my job search. I realized that pursuing it too aggressively might lead to a delayed response on the other end."

"So, you are jobless!"

People neglect what they can do and try to focus on what they cannot do. That's why the Bible says in Proverbs 26:16 (KJV) "The sluggard *is* wiser in his own conceit than seven men that can render a reason."

In other words, a lazy man can outwit seven people that come to convince him about his laziness. Seven! Not five or six! A lazy man will outwit seven people who tell him he should not be on his bed on Monday morning at 9:00 A.M. He thinks he is trying to strategize which application to fill out. You need to make a decision.

Don't fail in school before you decide to make a change. How many more subjects will you fail before you know it is time to change your inner circle?

Take Control of Your Destiny

Your friends don't have to be good-looking. They just have to be good-thinking. Ten or fifteen years from now those good-looking friends will be irrelevant.

I love to talk to people. Some of them are doing amazing things, but they are so quiet that you would never suspect it. They have taken leaps and bounds. It may be with college or with their work.

In five or ten years, you won't be able to recognize some people you go to church with. You have been hearing the same word they hear. How many opportunities for promotion will you pass up? How many more years will you neglect your relationship with God?

Inertia is the force that prevents initiation of a new action. It is also the force that keeps the old action in place, resisting any change in direction. People fear the next step, thinking *"what if it is worse than where I am?"*

The prodigal son did not let fear stop him from making a move. Do you know why President Trump became the president? He ran for office! You may think you are so smart, but what are *you* doing? He is the president today because he ran.

Say to yourself, "I am going somewhere. I am going to make a change." Instead of complaining, say to yourself *"Why am I sitting here until I die?"* More people need to run for office.

God is for you, who can be against you?

Joshua was not afraid.

> *No man shall be able to stand before you all the days of your life; as I was with Moses, so I will be with you. I will not leave you nor forsake you. Be strong and of good courage, for to this people you shall divide as an inheritance the land which I*

The Power of a New Beginning

swore to their fathers to give them. Joshua 1:5-6 NKJV

God spoke to me and said, "Your victory is on the other side of your fear" (*Seize Your Moment: Unmasking Everyday Opportunities*) Don't wait for fear to leave. Sometimes you have to go forward in the face of fear.

Finally, he took action. He went in the right direction. He became aware of the pigs. He asked himself the question. There was holy discontent. He evaluated. He made a decision. The next thing it says is, "He arose."

You need to walk towards your promise. You need to take steps in a new direction. Many have made a decision yet failed to act. They became aware they were discontented. They convinced themselves it was not the right time.

Do something that is in your power right now. Ecclesiastes 11:4 (TLB) says, "If you wait for perfect conditions, you will never get anything done."

The New King James Version says, "He who observes the wind will not sow, and he who regards the clouds will not reap."

An unknown author said, "Go where you are celebrated - not tolerated."[3]

He acted on his decision. He went to his father, and the reception was more than he anticipated. He must have had all kinds of reasons in his mind why he should not have gone. These giants in his mind did not stop him.

When I decided to write my first book, I stayed motivated for a while. Then, motivation lessened. My wife finally said, "You need to finish that book." I decided to finish it.

I didn't know what to do next or who I should take it to. I went to a book signing later, bought a book, and met the author. I asked him what I should do about my own book. He said he used Amazon. I discussed it with Amazon. That day I paid for their package. I knew I was hooked, because once I paid for publishing, I knew I would have to finish it or my money would be wasted. I had a deadline. I also wrote a workbook. The workbook went much faster! You need to have a goal.

When you sleep for twelve hours a day, you will have all these giants in your head, these reasons why you cannot go forward. II Kings 7:3-8 discusses the four leprous men sitting at the gate:

> *Now there were four leprous men at the entrance of the gate; and they said to one another, "Why are we sitting here until we die? If we say, 'We will enter the city,' the famine is in the city, and we shall die there. And if we sit here, we die also. Now therefore, come, let us surrender to the army of the Syrians. If they keep us alive, we shall live; and if they kill us, we shall only die." And they rose at twilight to go to the camp of the Syrians; and when they had come to the outskirts of the Syrian camp, to their surprise no one was there. For the Lord had caused the army of the Syrians to hear the noise of chariots and the noise of horses—the noise of a great army."* (God multiplied the sound of their footsteps, not the sound of their snoring.) *"...so they said to one another, "Look, the king of Israel has hired against us the kings of the Hittites and the kings of the Egyptians to attack us!" Therefore they arose and fled at twilight."* II Kings 7:3-8

The lepers decided to walk toward the possibility of life.

God said no man would be able to stand before you all the days of your life. If you are not standing, there is nothing for Him to remove. Examples of taking action or standing can be signing up for a course, doing research, applying for a job, or positioning yourself to take advantage of opportunities in the next few years.

> *In all labor there is profit, But idle chatter leads only to poverty.* Proverbs 14:23

The next step may be rekindling a relationship or making a fresh commitment to one. It may be tuning out people you recognize as hindrances to your calling or returning to a church you have disconnected from.

Return to God and accept God's invitation to return to a relationship with Him. The story of the prodigal son is really about the Father's love for us. It says in Luke 15:20 "…when he was still a great way off, his father saw him and had compassion, and ran and fell on his neck and kissed him." His father was lovingly waiting for him to come back. Don't be afraid to walk back to what God has promised you.

Take a step towards the future God has prepared for you. Take control of your destiny!

Prayer to Receive Jesus Christ as Your Lord and Savior

Father, thank You for sending Your Son, Jesus Christ, to die for me on the cross. I believe in my heart that Jesus is the Son of God, that He died on the cross, and that He rose again from the dead. I confess that He is my Lord and Savior. I commit my life to You; come into my life and be my Lord and Savior.

In Jesus' name,

Amen

End Notes

Chapter 1
[1] Monroe, Myles. *Maximizing Your Potential*. Shippensburg, PA: Destiny Image, Inc. 2011. Epub.
[2] Osteen, Joel. "Joel Osteen Quotes." BrainyQuote.com. Xplore Inc, 2018.

Chapter 3
[1] Clark, Scott. "The Old Engineer and the Hammer." Buzzmaven. Buzzmaven.com. January 2014. Google.

Chapter 4
[1] Ward, Arthur. "Three Enemies of Personal Peace. " Quotefancy. Quotefancy.com. 2018. Google.

Chapter 5
[1] "Discipline." Dictionary.com. 2018.
http://www.dictionary.com/browse/discipline?s=t (12 July 2018)

[2] Bulwer-Lytton, Edward G. "Genius Does What it Must, and Talent Does What it Can." BrainyQuote. BrainyQuote.com. 2018. Google.

Chapter 7
[1] Prochnow, Herbert. "There is a time when we must firmly choose the course." BrainyQuote.com. 2018. Google.

[2] Oyedepo, David. "Stages." Fresh Words Inspired. Freshwordsinspired.tumblr.com. 2018. Google.
[3] Author unknown. "Go where you are celebrated, not tolerated." Jeremy McCaslin. 2014. Google.

About the Author

'Lanre Somorin MD is a board-certified psychiatrist and has been practicing since 1995. He is also an associate pastor. He has a specialty in Addiction Psychiatry.

Somorin's mission is to help people discover hope and to live purposeful lives. Somorin is the medical director for an outpatient mental health facility with seven clinical sites.

He has been listed in the Top Doctors' issue of the Hudson Valley (NY) Magazine yearly since 2006. He owned and operated an outpatient substance abuse rehab facility and has held various leadership positions, including clinical consultant to the Army Substance Abuse Clinic in West Point, NY. He has a private behavioral health practice in Monroe, NY. He is married and is the father of two.

Seize Your Moment

In *Seize Your Moment (Unmasking Everyday Opportunities)*, board-certified psychiatrist and associate pastor 'Lanre Somorin, MD, reveals thirty-one keys to overcoming the barriers that prevent us from capitalizing on what daily life has to offer. Combining scripture with practical tools, motivational quotes, and insightful advice, Somorin empowers readers to take full control of their lives.

Starting with the vital role preparation plays in identifying and taking advantage of opportunities, Somorin explores the need for understanding and wisdom, tips for dealing with adversity, and the importance of removing distractions. You'll discover how the simplest ideas often represent opportunity and recognize that successfully capitalizing on opportunity does not mean avoiding hard work.

www.seizeyourmomentnow.com

www.ingramcontent.com/pod-product-compliance
Lightning Source LLC
LaVergne TN
LVHW051510070426
835507LV00022B/3032